# YOURS TILL BANANA SPLITS

# YOURS TILL
# BANANA SPLITS

## 201 AUTOGRAPH RHYMES

COMPILED BY
## JOANNA COLE
AND
## STEPHANIE CALMENSON

ILLUSTRATED BY
## ALAN TIEGREEN

A Beech Tree Paperback Book
New York

The Library of Congress has cataloged the Morrow Junior Books edition of
*Yours Till Banana Splits* as follows:
Cole, Joanna.
Yours till banana splits: 201 autograph rhymes/by Joanna Cole and Stephanie Calmenson;
illustrated by Alan Tiegreen.
p. cm.
Summary: A collection of rhymes suitable for writing in autograph books.
1. Children's poetry—Collections.   2. Humorous poetry—Collections.   3. Autograph albums.
(1. American poetry—Collections.   2. Humorous poetry—Collections.   3. Autograph albums.)
I. Calmenson, Stephanie.   II. Tiegreen, Alan, ill.   III. Title.   PN6110.C6C615 1995
811'.54089282—dc20   94-10654   CIP   AC

First Beech Tree Edition, 1995.
ISBN 0-688-14019-X
1 3 5 7 9 10 8 6 4 2

# CONTENTS

# SIGN HERE, PLEASE!

When we set out to create a book of autograph rhymes, we knew we would need a little help from our friends. "Do you happen to have any of your autograph albums?" we asked. One by one, yearbooks and autograph albums appeared. Friends who had trouble finding their shoes in the morning were able to put their hands on their old albums in minutes. Some did not want to part with them. "You can only borrow it overnight." "Make sure you give it back." "Could you read it at my house?"

Our friends seemed happy to reread their albums, remembering their old pals and their old school days. We had fun reading them, too. We were surprised to find out which of our friends had been really popular, mischievous, boy crazy, or girl crazy. (Sometimes we weren't so surprised!)

We enjoyed reading the albums for other reasons as well. Some rhymes are funny. Some are touching. And all of them have rhythm and joy in the language.

There are rhymes about friendship, school, and romance. There are good wishes, predictions, and some insults, too. But the message we found repeated most often is: Remember *me*!

So use these rhymes to sign as many albums as you can.

That way, kids will remember *you*. And try to get as many signatures as you can in your own album. Someday you will have fun looking back at them.

By the way, don't forget to sign your own album. Who knows, you may become famous one day. Then you'll already have your autograph. Here's a rhyme you can use:

**Ha, ha, ha!**
**It makes me laugh**
**To sign my own autograph.**

_____
(sign your name)

# GO, LITTLE ALBUM

Get as many signatures as you can.
When you are older, you'll be glad you have them.

Go, little album, far and near,
To all my friends I hold so dear
And ask them each to write a page
That I may read in my old age.

# THERE'S NO SHIP LIKE FRIENDSHIP

Here are some special rhymes for your closest friends.

There are gold ships,
There are silver ships.
But there's no ship
Like friendship.

There's green tea, black tea,
Hot tea, iced tea.
But there's no tea
Like loyalty.

Tell me fast
Before I faint.
Is we friends
Or is we ain't?

Pals we are,
Pals we'll be,
Pals forever,
You and me.

Ashes to ashes,
Dust to dust.
You're one friend
That I can trust.

Peaches grow in Florida,
California, too.
But it takes a state like _____
(your state)
To grow a peach like you.

Friends are like melons—
I'll tell you why.
To find a good one,
A hundred you must try.

If I were a head of lettuce,
I'd cut myself in two.
I'd give the leaves to all my friends
And save the heart for you.

Some like three.
Some like two.
But I like one,
And that is you.

A ring is round and has no end. So is my love for you, my friend.

As long as two nickels make a dime,
You'll always be a friend of mine.

I like coffee,
I like tea.
I like you,
And you like me.

If you get to heaven
Before I do,
Bore a little hole
And pull me through.

It's bad to lose a friend
When your eyes are full of hope.
But it's worse to lose a towel
When your eyes are full of soap.

In your ocean of friends, please count me as a
permanent wave.

In your bracelet of friendship, consider me a link.

If anybody likes you more than me,
They will have to sign their name below mine.

# CAN'T THINK, BRAIN DUMB

When you can't think what to write,
try writing one of these.

Can't think,
Brain dumb,
Inspiration
Won't come.
Bad ink.
Worse pen.
Best wishes,
Amen.

I dip my pen into the ink
And grasp your album tight.
And for your sake I cannot find
A single word to write.

I've tried to think of something,
But my mind has fallen flat.
I'll say that you're a friend of mine
And let it go at that.

I thought, I thought, I thought in vain.
At last I thought I'd sign my name.

You asked me to sign my autograph,
But I'd rather have your photograph.
So let me know by telegraph
How you like my paragraph.

Some write for pleasure.
Some write for fame.
But I write only
To sign my name.

Some people are naughty.
Some people are nice.
I will be naughty
And sign my name twice.

I have no poem
To write just now,
But I wish you good luck
Anyhow.

It tickles me,
It makes me laugh
To think you want
My autograph.

Round went the album,
Hither it came,
For me to write,
So here's my name.

I can't give you fortune,
I can't give you fame.
I can only help fill
This book with my name.

## UPSIDE DOWN
## (AND ROUND AND ROUND)
Some of us just have to do things our own way.

I bet you I can make any fool in town
Turn this album upside down.

Two in a hammock
Ready to kiss
When all of a sudden
It goes like this!

As years roll on,
And roll they will,
Remember your friend
Who wrote uphill.

I'm the toughest in the city,
I'm the toughest in the town.
I'm the one who spoiled your book
By writing upside down.

When on this page you look,
When on this page you frown,
Remember the one who spoiled it
By writing upside down.

I am a nut,
I am a clown.
That's why I signed
Upside down.

Roses are red,

green grow the hedges. I think I'll write around the edges.

Health. Happiness. Success. Wealth.

Hope you hit a home run!

I
I did
I did this
I did this to
I did this to take
I did this to take up
I did this to take up space.


| Read | see | that | me. |
|------|-----|------|-----|
| up | will | I | like |
| and | you | like | you |
| down | and | you | and |

Some write up and some write down, but I'll be different and write around.

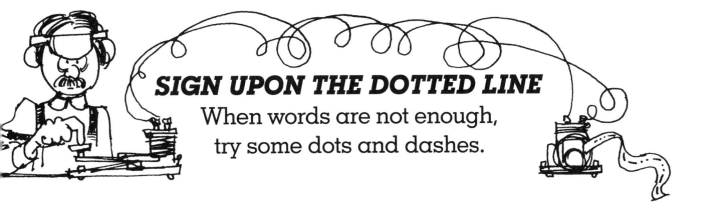

## SIGN UPON THE DOTTED LINE
When words are not enough,
try some dots and dashes.

In this book I'll gladly sign
Right upon the dotted line.

- - - - - - - - - - - - - - - - - - - - - - -

Four lines from a lazy poet:

_____

_____

_____

_____

•Dot
●Blot
Forget-me-not.

# ROSES ARE RED, VIOLETS ARE BLUE
Keep reading to see what they say about you.

Roses are red,
Violets are blue.
Sugar is sweet
And so are you.

Roses are red,
Violets are blue.
God made me handsome.
What happened to you?

Roses are red,
Violets are blue.
Lend me ten dollars
And I will love you.

Roses are red,
Violets are blue.
The ASPCA
Is looking for you.

Satellites are red,
Rockets are blue.
If you don't behave,
I'll send you up, too.

Roses are red,
Violets are blue.
How the heck
Did you get through?

Roses are red,
Violets are blue.
When it rains,
I'll think of you.
*Drip. Drip. Drip.*

Roses are red,
Violets are blue.
If you were my honey,
I'd kiss you.

Roses are red,
Violets are black.
How I will laugh
When you get left back.

Roses are red,
Violets are blue.
What you need
Is a good shampoo.

Roses are red,
Violets are blue.
R U 4 me?
I M 4 U.

# OPEN IF YOU DARE

How about some secret-message autographs?

Fold the page in half, as shown, and try writing some of these messages.

**1. On the outside of a folded page, write:**
For dirty people only

**2. On the inside, write:**
A song in four bars—
Soap! Soap! Soap! Soap!

**1. On the outside of a folded page in a boy's book, write:**
For girls only

**2. On the inside, write:**
I've got your attention.
Now listen to this:
If you are reading this page,
You must give _____ a kiss.
(name of book's owner)

**1. On the outside of a folded page in a girl's book, write:**
For boys only

**2. On the inside, write:**
Whoever here may chance to look
Must kiss the owner of this book.

**1. On the outside of a folded page, write:**
DO NOT LOOK UNDER THIS FLAP!

**2. On the inside, write:**
You're not very good at
 following directions, are you?
Have a great life anyway!

1. *In the center of an open page, draw a picture of a*
   *four-leaf clover. To the right of the picture, write:*
   **You opened this page**
   **And the meaning is plain—**
   **Seven years of good luck**
   **Are yours to gain.**

2. *Fold the page over so that half*
   *the four-leaf clover is covered.*
   *Write on the outside flap:*
   **Open if you dare!**

## HERE'S ONE MORE SECRET-MESSAGE AUTOGRAPH:

1. *Write this verse on the page near the binding of the book, so it can be read when the page is folded.*

   If you can't read
   What I wrote in your book,
   Fold down the page
   And take another look.

2. *Now fold over one-fourth of the page.*

3. *Then write a message like this, so that half the message goes on the page and half ends up on the folded-over part:*

G
O
O
D

L
U
C
K

**4. When you finish writing, unfold the page. It will look like this:**

**5. Your friend has to fold the page again to read your message.**

## ON THIS PAGE OF PINKY PINK

Why do you think autograph books
have colored pages?
So you'll have something to write about, of course.

On this page of pinky pink
I write my name in inky ink.

On this page of pinky pink
I write my name in stinky ink.
I wish that I could write in gold
But ink is all my pen can hold.

May your life be as rosy as this page.

I write upon this page of blue.
May your fondest wish come true.
Oh, my gosh, erase the ink!
I take it back, the page is pink!

On this page of bluey blue
It looked so good I took a chew.

I write upon this page of blue
To wish success in all you do.

May you never feel like the color of this page.

On this page
Of whitey white
I'm the one
Who dares to write.

I'll write on white
To be polite
And I'll leave the yellow
For your fellow.

If this page were pretty pink,
I would have to say you stink.
But the page is whitey white
So I can say you are all right.




On this page so clean and white
It looked so good I took a bite.

Oh, my go
I take it back,

I've signed my name
On this green page
For you to read
In your old age.

Green is the color I like best.
You are the one I wish success.

Green are the leaves,
Green is the stem,
Green is this page,
Best wishes, amen.

# *YOURS TILL...*
Here's how to spell out your never-ending
devotion to your friends.

**Yours till soda pops.**

**Yours till meat balls bounce.**

**Yours till bacon strips.**

**Yours till butter flies.**

**Yours till ginger snaps.**

**Yours till banana splits.**

**Yours till ice screams.**

Yours till the mouth of the Mississippi wears lipstick.

Yours till Niagara Falls.

Yours till Bear Mountain gets dressed.

Yours till Catskill mountains.

Yours till Dracula stops being a pain in the neck.

Yours till cereal bowls.

Yours till the kitchen sinks.

Yours till the ocean wears rubber pants to keep its bottom dry.

Yours till the board walks.

Yours till the fire escapes.

Yours till the bed spreads.

Yours till the whipped cream peaks and sees the salad dressing.

Yours till the comic strips.

Yours till the pencil case is solved.

Yours till the tree barks.

# TEACHER'S PET

It's time to remember the good old days in school.

Remember the fork.
Remember the spoon.
Remember the fun
We had in homeroom.

Remember the A.
Remember the B.
Remember the day
We both got a D.

Remember the fights.
Remember the fun.
Remember the homework
That never got done.

Don't you worry.
Don't you fret.
We can't all be
Teacher's pet.

Up the river,
Down the lake.
Teacher's got
A bellyache.

Sitting in the schoolroom
Chewing bubble gum.
In walks the principal,
Out comes the gum.

Hit 'em in the head.
Hit 'em in the feet.
We've got a class
That can't be beat.

Now I lay me down to rest.
I pray I'll pass tomorrow's test.
If I die before I wake,
That's one less test
I'll have to take.

Poor little _____
(name of book's owner)
Sitting on a fence,
Trying to get to high school
Without any sense.

Friends, Romans, countrymen,
Lend me your homework.

# LOOK WHO'S GRADUATING!
### You made it!

Friends, Romans, countrymen,
Lend me your ears.
Look who's graduating
After all these years.

2, 4, 6, 8,
How the heck did you graduate?

Come out of your coma
And get your diploma.

Lucky _____ is getting a rest.
(old school)
Too bad _____ is getting a pest.
(new school)

Get ahead in high school.
(You'll need one.)

Roses are red,
Violets are blue.
What a relief
To get rid of you.

Birds on the mountain,
Fish in the sea.
How you ever graduated
Is a mystery to me.

Open the gate!
Open the gate!
Here comes _____,
(name of book's owner)
The graduate.

Graduation, graduation,
See you at the Greyhound station.

# I LOVE YOU ONCE, I LOVE YOU TWICE

Here are some lovey-dovey autographs
for that special someone.

I love you once,
I love you twice.
I love you next to
Beans and rice.

I love you, I love you,
I love you divine.
Please give me your gum—
You're sitting on mine.

Pigs love pumpkins.
Cows love squash.
I love you,
I do, by gosh.

If you think you are in love
And still there is some question,
Don't worry much about it—
It may be indigestion.

You drink a lot of soda.
You eat a lot of cream.
But when you get older,
You'll be someone's dream.

Do you love me
Or do you not?
You told me once,
But I forgot.

He kissed you by the garden.
Your mother heard the SMACK.
She got so very, very mad
She made you give it back.

Don't kiss boys
By the garden gate.
Love is blind,
But the neighbors ain't.

There are tulips in the garden,
There are tulips in the park.
But the best tulips of all
Are the two lips that meet in the dark.

Never let a kiss fool you.
And never let a fool kiss you.

Girls are like a nugget of gold—
Hard to get and hard to hold.

Little Jack Horner sat in a corner
Watching _____ go by.
(girl's name)
He thought she was a beauty
And said, "Come here, cutie."
That's how he got his black eye.


If there were a girls' camp
Across the sea,
What a great swimmer
_____ would be.
(boy's name)

Bread and butter,
Sugar and spice.
Lots of girls
Think you're nice.

You be the ice cream,
I'll be the freezer.
You be the lemon,
I'll be the squeezer.

Your head is like a ball of straw.
Your nose is long and funny.
Your mouth is like a cellar door.
But still I love you, honey.

Tables are round.
Chairs are square.
You and _____
Make a good pair.

Love is a feeling that you feel
When you feel you are going to feel
A feeling you've never felt before.

Butter is butter.
Cheese is cheese.
What's a kiss
Without a squeeze?

To kiss a miss is awfully simple.
To miss a kiss is simply awful.

You love yourself, you think you're grand.
You go to the movies and hold your hand.
You put your arm around your waist
And when you get fresh, you slap your face.

# WHEN YOU GET MARRIED...

Just think, you can invite all the kids who signed
your autograph book to your wedding.

When you get married
And live in a tree,
Send me a coconut
C.O.D.

When you get married
And your honey gets cross,
Stand up and say,
"Who made *you* boss?"

When Cupid shoots
His golden arrow,
I hope he "Mrs." you.

If you get married
And have a divorce,
Come to my stable
And marry my horse.

2 little lovebirds,
little kisses,
weeks later, Mr. and Mrs.

When you get married
And live on a hill,
Send me a kiss
By the whippoorwill.

When you get married
And live in a hut,
Send me a picture
Of each little nut.

When you get married
And you have twins,
Just call on me
For safety pins.

When you are courting,
It's honey and pie.
But when you get married,
It's root, hog, or die.

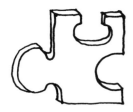

# U R 2 NICE

Can you puzzle these out?

U R
2 nice
2 B
4-gotten


2 Y's U R
2 Y's U B
I C U R
2 Y's 4 me.

Never
2 young
2 go
4 boys

U R A Q T.
I N V U.

Hint: Another word for *car* is *auto*.

# DON'T THINK YOU'RE SO COOL

These insults really aren't very nice.
But what's an autograph book without 'em?

Just because your head is shaped like an air
conditioner, don't think you're so cool.

Sugar is sweet.
Coal is black.
Do me a favor
And sit on a tack.

My house is near a pond.
Drop in sometime.

Don't worry—the Liberty Bell is cracked, too.

Pickles cost money,
Pickles are green.
My face is funny,
But yours is a scream.

If in heaven we don't meet,
I hope that you can stand the heat.

Calling car 1!
Calling car 2!
_____ and _____
Just escaped from the zoo.

When you are sick
And going to die,
Call me up
And I will cry.

I love you, I love you
With my heart and soul.
If I had a doughnut,
I'd give you the hole.

I love you, I love you,
I love you so well,
If I had a peanut,
I'd give you the shell.

I love you, I love you,
I love you, I do.
But don't get excited—
I love monkeys, too.

Roses are red,
Grass is green.
Take my advice.
Use Listerine.

Roses are red,
They grow in this region.
If I had your face,
I'd join the Foreign Legion.

Roses are red,
Violets are blue.
Umbrellas get lost,
Why don't you?

# REMEMBER ME...
Isn't this what autograph books are all about?

Remember Grant,
Remember Lee.
But most of all,
Remember ME.

Remember A,
Remember B.
But C that U
Remember me.

Remember me once,
Remember me twice.
Remember the one
Who thinks you're nice.

Remember me now,
Remember me ever.
Remember the fun
We had together.

When you stand upon the stump,
Think of me before you jump.

When you see a monkey up a tree,
Pull his tail and think of me.

If scribbling in albums
Remembrance insures,
With the greatest of pleasure
I scribble in yours.

In my garden there is a rock
On which it says, "Forget me not."
In my garden there is a tree
On which it says, "Remember me."

Remember the gate,
Remember the spot.
Remember the flower
Forget-me-not.

There are walnuts,
There are peanuts.
But the best nuts
Are forget-me-nuts.

Remember the M,
Remember the E.
Put them together—
Remember ME.

What! Write in your album?
What shall it be?
Just two little words,
"Remember me."

Forget the moon, forget the stars.
Forget to flirt on trolley cars.
Forget your holey socks to mend.
But don't forget your good old friend.

When you get old
And cannot see,
Put on your specs
And think of me.

# MAY YOUR LIFE BE...

When you want to wish your friends the very best,
try one of these.

May your life be like toilet paper—
Long and useful.

May your life be like spaghetti—
Long and full of dough.

May your life be like arithmetic—
Joys added.
Sorrows subtracted.
Friends multiplied.
Love undivided.

May your life be bright and sunny
And your husband fat and funny.

Best of luck in all you do.
I hope your wishes all come true.

I hope you will be famous.
I hope you'll be a star.
I hope you get a really great
Big red car.

I hope you climb this ladder:

**L**
ots of
uck in
ove and
ife.
ove and best wishes.

May you always sit in this chair:

I wish you a succession of successful successes.

Good better best—
Never let it rest
Until the good is better
And the better's best.

Take the local,
Take the express,
But don't get off
Till you reach success.

Sit on the tack of success
And you will surely rise.

May your joys be as deep as the ocean
And your sorrows as light as the foam.

A wise old owl sat in an oak.
The more he saw, the less he spoke.
The less he spoke, the more he heard.
Just try to be like that old bird.

Let the first letter
Of each of these lines
Vanish all the troubles
Ever in your mind.

## *THE END*

The last page in an autograph book, like the first,
is a special one. Who will get to sign last?

Like Oliver Twist, I'm last on the list.

By hook or by crook,
I'll be last in this book.

By eggs or by bacon,
You're sadly mistaken.

Sorry, my friend.
*I'm* at the end.

# WHERE TO FIND MORE

## SOME SOURCES FOR AUTOGRAPH RHYMES

Emrich, Duncan. *The Hodgepodge Book*. New York: Four Winds, 1972.

——. *The Whim-Wham Book*. New York: Four Winds, 1975.

Morrison, Lillian. *Best Wishes, Amen: A New Collection of Autograph Verses*. New York: HarperCollins Children's Books, 1989.

——. *Remember Me When This You See*. New York: Thomas Y. Crowell, 1961.

——, ed. *Yours Till Niagara Falls: A Book of Autograph Verses*. New York: HarperCollins Children's Books, 1990.

Opie, Iona, and Peter Opie. *I Saw Esau*. Cambridge, Massachusetts: Candlewick, 1992.

Withers, Carl. *A Rocket in My Pocket: The Rhymes and Chants of Young Americans*. New York: Henry Holt, 1988.